The Project LETTERING BOOK

Robert Ainsworth

SCHOLASTIC INC.

New York Toronto London Auckland Sydney
Mexico City New Delhi Hong Kong

Dedicated to my five children,
Nadan, Lara, Rowan, Merribeth and Bronton,
who contributed some of the ideas for this book.

ISBN 0-439-10844-6

12 11 10 9 8 7 6 5 4 3 2   0 1 2 3 4/0

Printed in the U.S.A.   08

First Scholastic printing, October 1999

Typeset by Proset Imaging, Forresters Beach NSW.

CONTENTS

About this Book

The idea for this book was born in a classroom while I was preparing a spelling lesson for a group of Year 7 students.

I doctored-up the words a bit to make them look like what they meant.

The students were excited about what we could do with words—just by using a bit of imagination and having a sense of fun.

I'm sure you will be as excited as they were!

In this book I've given you lots of examples to help you get started.

HAVE FUN! Robert Ainsworth

These are the twelve 'dull and boring' words which I had to teach to my Year 7 class. Here are the original ideas I used to bring the words to life, to try to make the task of remembering what they meant—and how to spell them—easier.

 **NOW...**

Let's try some simple words— straight out of the Dictionary.

- BABY
- BAD
- BADGE
- BAG
- BAKE
- BALANCE
- BALD
- BALE
- BALL
- BALLOON
- BAMBOO
- BANANA
- BANG
- BANK
- BANNER

Let's see what we can do with them...

I wonder how much we can do with **ONE** *word....?*

We'll need to pick a word that reminds us of lots of things.

Let's see .... **BEACH!** *That's a good word.*

There are lots of things to see at the seaside.
We can use them to take the place of some of the letters in the word "BEACH."

Things like...

Here we go... B**each** BEACH BEACH

Beach BEACH BEACH

Beach BEACH BEACH

BEACH BEACH BEACH

Beach BEACH BEACH

BEACH BEACH BEACH

BEACH Beach

BEACH Beach Beach

As you can see... the sky is the limit with what you can do with words!

9

Here are some C's...

- CAB
- CABBAGE
- CABIN
- CABLE
- CACTUS
- CAGE
- CAKE
- CAMP

HOSE   DIFFERENT

TRAP   CLOMP

LEAF   DISAPPEAR   ROOF

WOOL   ARTIST   Puddle

GOLF   IGNITE   STRICT

SIGN   WHEELS   BUMPED

Travel   Grab   EAGLE   FLY

Here's a **FUN** word!

14

Let's do some **Face**

EXPRESSION words...

Happy SAD GROWL

FROWN Lough CRY

Grump Groan Asleep

scowl Grin SHOUT

FLIRT smile BLOW

chew Bite cringe

How about **BODY PARTS...**

Head NOSE SKULL

FACE NOSE eyes

MOUTH cheeks chin

Tongue TEETH ears

Beard Neck Hair

More... **BODY PARTS**

LIPS Freckles HAIR

Jaw Moustache HAIR

TOE FEET Leg

TUMMY ANKLE BOTTOM

ARM Brain BONE

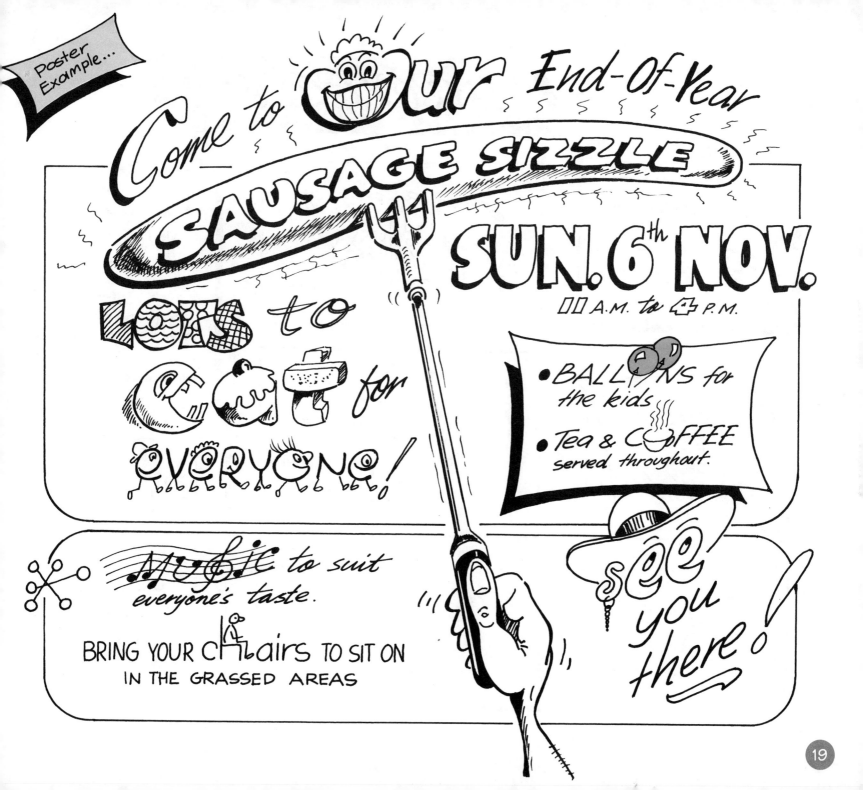

... FOR PROJECTS

AMERICA

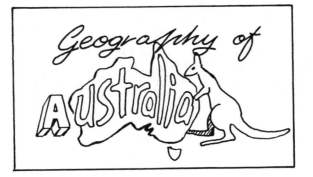

Geography of Australia

MY VISIT TO PARIS

FISH OF The World

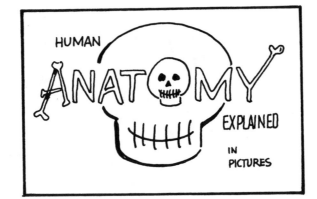

HUMAN ANATOMY EXPLAINED IN PICTURES

OUR EXCURSION TO THE BEACH

MOUNTAIN RANGES IN ASIA

SOME OF THE BIG ANIMALS OF THE WORLD

WOOL GROWING in New Zealand

A good way to come up with ideas for your project title is to think of the OBJECTS the title reminds you of.

 *For example...*

IN THIS CASE THE **OBJECT** IS THE SHEAF OF WHEAT — BUT NOTICE ALSO THE BIRDS AND CLOUDS WHICH ADD ATMOSPHERE.

You can even make the whole word into an object.

 *For example...*

AGAIN... ADD THE SUN AND BIRDS AND HORIZON. THESE HELP TO ESTABLISH A SENSE OF PLACE.

Another very good way to generate ideas is to think of the ACTION the title reminds you of.

 *For example...*

HARVEST

Don't forget, you can turn the letters into **BODY PARTS**.

This can be very useful because body parts — or even whole bodies — can portray **ACTION** as well.

Examples...

You can even use animals...

Put your ideas to good USE FOR SIGNS ...

Buy your HOT CHIPS at the ...

Canteen

Tea and Coffee

50¢ a cup

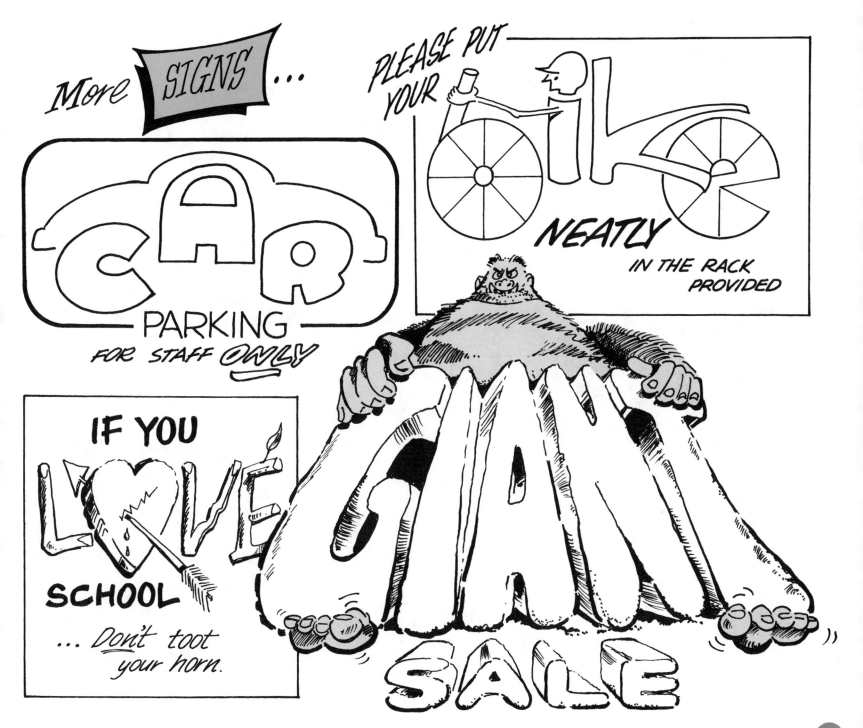

SIGNZ ...

Buy your BALLOONS HERE

Don't CLOWN around in this Room!

See you at the... Fotball CARNIVAL

Pick up your DIRTY SOX

Signs

WAVE Goodbye to HOMEWORK!
...See you at the GRADUATION DANCE

SWING TO THE BEAT...
at the
BIG BAND BASH!

Welcome to the...

HARVEST MOON DANCE

maGic TRIX
INTERNATIONAL ®
Available for PARTIES
PROP: MADGE IKK.

Try some...

GEOMETRY Terms

ROUND   SQUARE   OBLONG

OVAL   TRIANGLE   DOT

PYRAMID   Hexagon

BLOCK   Parallelogram

CONE   DIAMOND   RHOMBUS

TRAPESIUM   PENTAGON

NOW Grab a pencil and paper and see what FUN ideas you can come up with for these

Business Names...

Example... • BUSY BEE HONEY Co

Busy Bee Honey Co.

Example... • FAST TRANSPORT Co

FAST TRANSPORT Co.

Example... • SWIMMING POOL Co

Swimming POOL Co.

NOTE: THERE ARE NO "RIGHT" WAYS OF DOING IT.

• SNAKE CHARMER

• VIDEO GAMES

• ROCK BANDS UNITED

• TOY SHOP

Don't Forget... You can use UPPER OR lower case letters

Turn over for more examples...

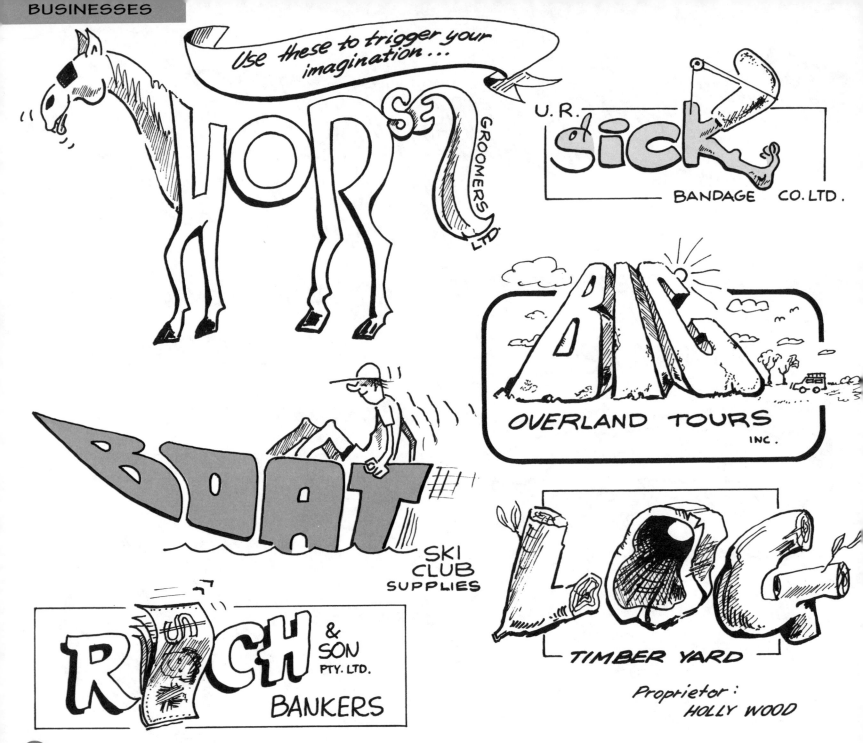

Use these to trigger your imagination...

HORSE GROOMERS LE

U.R. SICK BANDAGE CO. LTD.

BIG OVERLAND TOURS INC.

BOAT SKI CLUB SUPPLIES

LOG TIMBER YARD

Proprietor: HOLLY WOOD

RICH & SON PTY. LTD. BANKERS

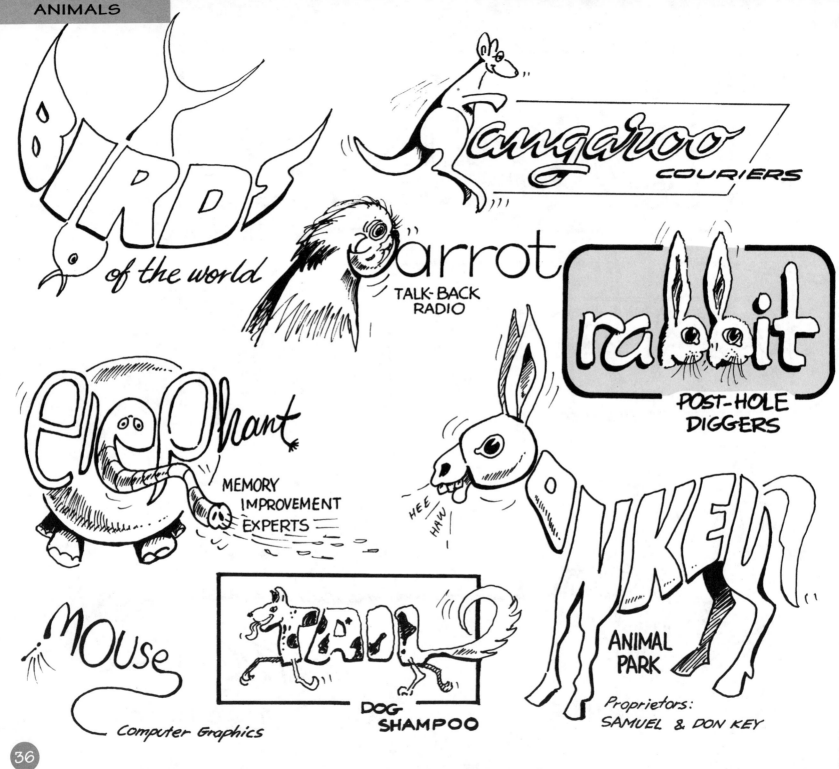

BIRDS of the world

Kangaroo COURIERS

Parrot
TALK-BACK RADIO

rabbit
POST-HOLE DIGGERS

elephant
MEMORY IMPROVEMENT EXPERTS

HEE HAW

DONKEY
ANIMAL PARK
Proprietors: SAMUEL & DON KEY

MOUSE
Computer Graphics

TAIL
DOG SHAMPOO

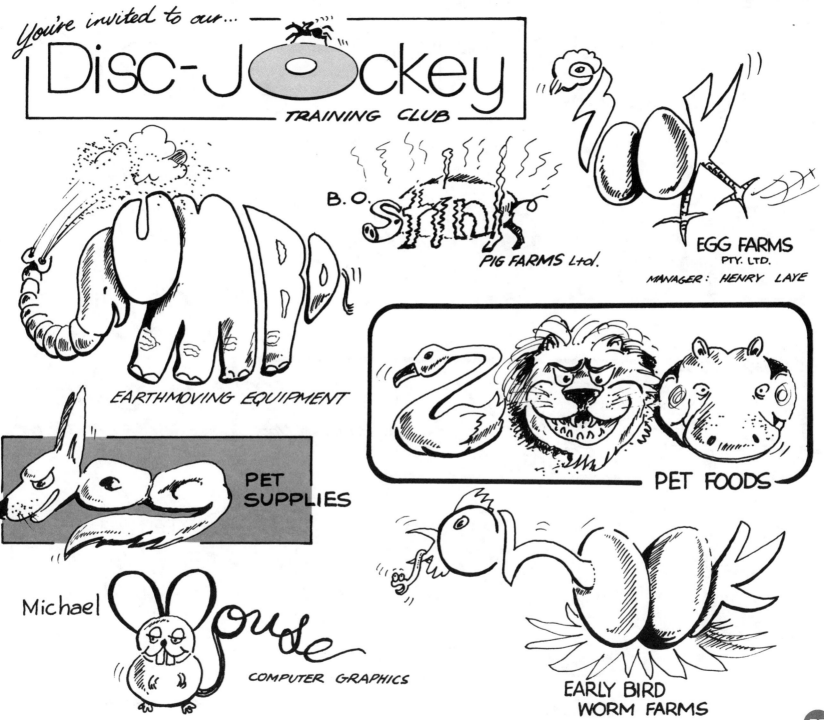

You're invited to our...

Disc-Jockey
TRAINING CLUB

EARTHMOVING EQUIPMENT

B.O. shnk
PIG FARMS Ltd.

EGG FARMS
PTY. LTD.
MANAGER: HENRY LAYE

PET
SUPPLIES

PET FOODS

Michael Mouse
COMPUTER GRAPHICS

EARLY BIRD
WORM FARMS

37

Prop: M.UNCH

Vineyard

WINE - TASTING

Take-away **FOOD**

Proprietor: M.T. TUMM

FUNNY "HA-HA

Cafe

PROP: PHYLLIS UPP

LEAVE YOUR

FAST FOOD

Prop.: Harry Upp.

ICECREAM Cº

PROPRIETORS:
PHILIP & ANITA.

TOFFEE

LOLLIE SHOP

Lunch BAR

Prop: Sam Vich.

COOK up a Feast with...

BANANA MONKEY BUSINESS FOODS

See you at the... SALT & peppACHOOO...

Restaurant FOR HOME-STYLE COOKING

D. LISIOUS Fruit & Vegies CO. LTD.

E. CLAIR baker PASTRYCOOK

coffee shop Prop: Mr Bean

Dinah's CUTLERY Carvery

Eat LUNCH BAR

E.T. Lollies! TOOTHBRUSH CO.

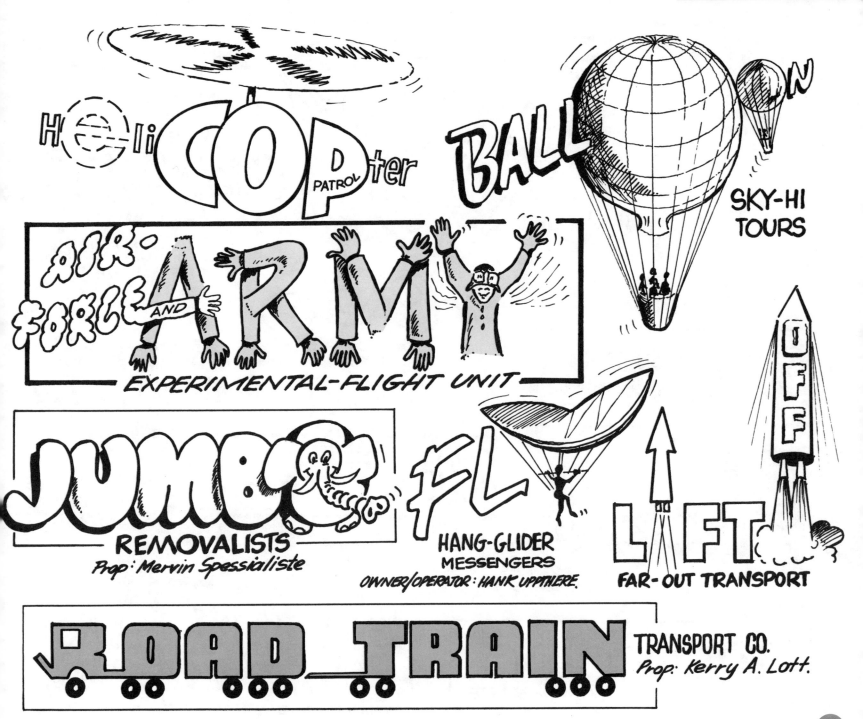

HEliCOPter
PATROL

BALLOON
SKY-HI TOURS

AIR-FORCE AND ARMY
EXPERIMENTAL-FLIGHT UNIT

JUMBO REMOVALISTS
Prop: Mervin Spessialiste

FLY
HANG-GLIDER MESSENGERS
OWNER/OPERATOR: HANK UPPTHERE.

LIFT OFF
FAR-OUT TRANSPORT

ROAD TRAIN TRANSPORT CO.
Prop: Kerry A. Lott.

41

BUTCHER

PRICE CUTTERS*

* WE'LL MEAT YOU HALF WAY.

Bell

CAR THIEF ALARMS

"tuuin" w.

& PARTNER

Double Agents

FRIDGE

WAR NEGOTIATORS
PEACE

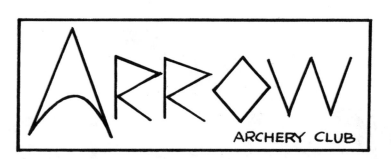

ARROW

ARCHERY CLUB

GANG

LINK ARMS FOR PEACE

CROSS

WORD PUZZLES INC.

PHOBIA ASSOCIATION INC.
PRESIDENT: A. FRED OVEVRITHING.

DENTIST VISIT
O. PENN-WYDE M.D.
IN ASSOCIATION WITH
I. HERCHEW T.E.Th.

COMMUNICATION SYSTEMS

Comical NOVELTY CO.
Manager: JOE KERR

STIRRERS INTERNATIONAL Inc.

OPTIMISTS CLUB!
PRESIDENT: GINGER (BLUE) SKYES.

GR**O**WL
COMPLAINTS
DEPARTMENT
Manager : LIONEL PHYTBACH

Grin
PHOTOGRAPHERS
CLUB
PRESIDENT : MONA LISA.

I.M. **Grumpy** & Co.
INSOMNIA CONSULTANTS

argue
U. & I. and Company

V**O**LC**A**N**O**

ANGER MANAGEMENT CONSULTANTS
MANAGER : HELEN BACK

E.T. **feed** & ASSOC.
APPETITE RESTORERS

A.

ner

BOUNDARY RIDER.

I.M. **ANGRY** & ASSOC.

PROTEST MARCHERS
CONGLOMERATE

slurp SOUP CO.

S**A**D PESSIMISTS
ASSOCIATION

GROUP THERAPY
GUILD

Talk PHONE
SYSTEMS

YAK!
YAK!
YAK!

C.LEE **JOKE** & CO.
NOVELTIES

with Patrick Ortreat & Assoc.

M.T. **SOFA** PSYCHIATRISTS
MANAGER: LOLA BOUTE

I. **forbid** & CO.
CHILD PSYCHOLOGISTS

46

GLASS &co.

SMASH &
GRAB
SPECIALISTS

NICK YORWALLET

Fingers

& ACCOMPLICE

PICKPOCKETS

PRISONER

Penfriends Inc.

SHERLOCK

MAGNIFY

& PARTNER

PRIVATE DETECTIVES

X.X.

robber

& Partners

ANTIQUE
COLLECTORS
&
JEWELLERS

POLICE

'ere specialists

SHADOW

DETECTIVES & NIGHTWATCHMENS
CLUB

THIS BUILDING IS BEING WATCHED BY...

SECURITY

UNDER-ARM
DEODORANT

SECURITY
GUARDS

LIARS CLUB
Inc.

SECRETARY : IDA DOWNE

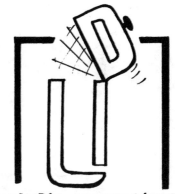

SCANDAL INVESTIGATORS
GUILD

FRED

Thread & Assoc.

PRIVATE DETECTIVES

IN ASSOCIATION WITH ESAU U. DOIT & CO.

BURGLAR ALARMS

SECURITY ALARMS

INSIDE-TUO

PRISONER REHABILITATION
SERVICES

49

Sea Gull HANG-GLIDER CLUB

FLOAT BANKERS

U. Can Swim & Co. SWIMMING CLASSES

SAVE the WHALES EAT YOUR VEGIES!

JAWS DIVING EQUIPMENT

diver STOCK MARKET PREDICTORS

Manager: Mark Ed. Krash.

LIGHTHOUSE MARINE

SAFETY PRODUCTS

Kissors Hairdressers

Hammer CARPENTERS

E.Z.

Curl HAIRDRESSERS

Manager: CARL E. LOCKE

Electricity Suppliers & Installers

Manager: S. PARK.

Will

Saweson CARPENTERS

Spot on-- Spot off

WINDOW CLEANERS

Snowman AIR-CONDITIONING EXPERTS

Harry

Beard BARBER

51

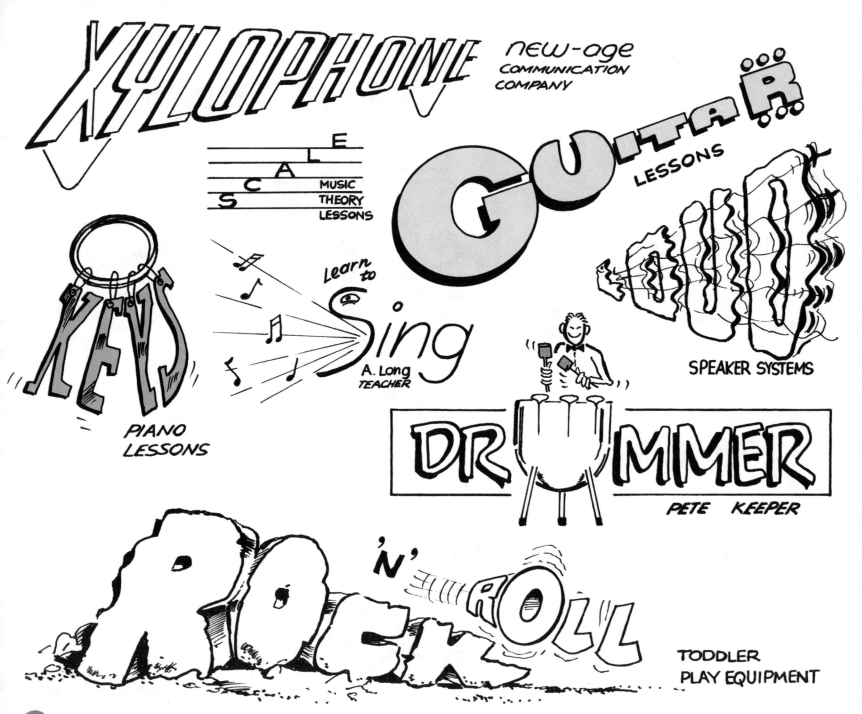

XYLOPHONE

NEW-AGE COMMUNICATION COMPANY

SCALE

MUSIC THEORY LESSONS

GUITAR

LESSONS

KEYS

PIANO LESSONS

Learn to Sing

A. Long
TEACHER

SPEAKER SYSTEMS

DRUMMER

PETE KEEPER

ROCK 'N' ROLL

TODDLER PLAY EQUIPMENT

BRUSH *Painters*
THEATRE BACKDROPS A SPECIALTY

ART Supplies

Hello STATUE?

Q.T. LIP STICK
COSMETIC MAKE-UP SERVICES

Tracy COMPASS DRAFTSPERSON

U. KEN DRAW & Co.
ART SUPPLIES

PAINTER & DECORATOR

T shirt
ADVERTISING AGENTS

53

HEADACHE

Soccer *Club*

COACH: O.F.F. SYDE

Tee Ball CLUB

DROWN

HOMEWORK HELPERS Inc.

CHARIOTEERING CLUB

LOOP

SLIPS

GYMNASTICS CLUB

JUMP

AEROBICS GROUP

INSTRUCTORS: HOWARD HIGH & JIM NASTIX

netball COACH: CHUCK INN
CLUB

HOOP
EXAM & TEST COACHERS
HEAD TEACHER: MARK HARD.

op-in Deli
Prop: Carmen U.R. Velcum

jaw
BOXING GLOVE
SUPPLIES

U.L.
slip
& Co.Ltd.
FLOOR POLISHERS

ouick COURIERS

Hit
SPORTS
EQUIPMENT

TIRED
FITNESS CLUB

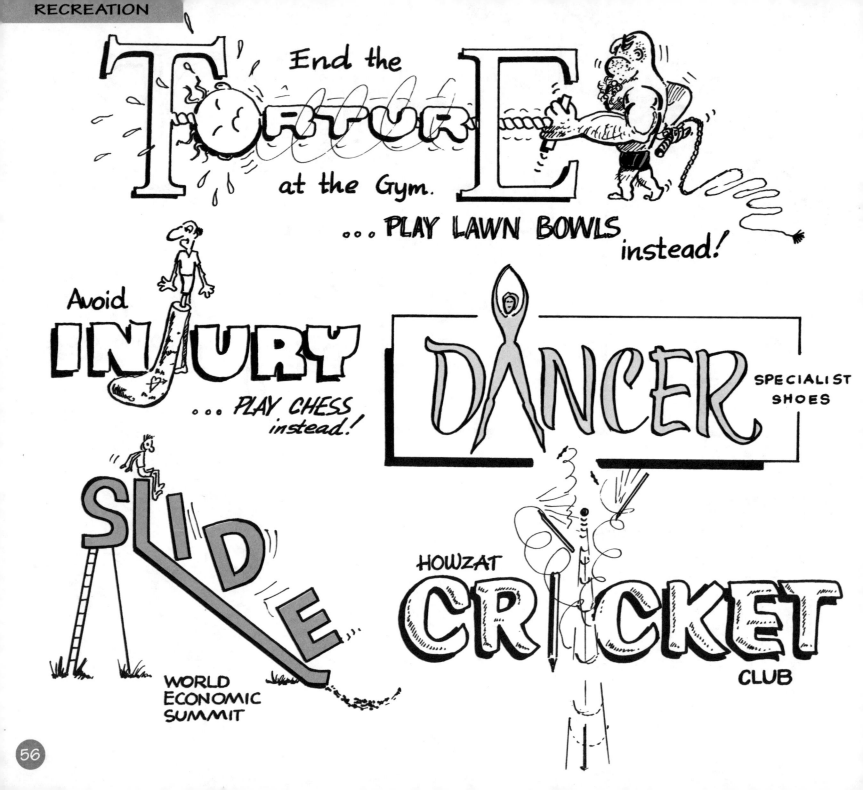

End the **TORTURE** at the Gym. ... PLAY LAWN BOWLS instead!

Avoid **INJURY** ... PLAY CHESS instead!

DANCER SPECIALIST SHOES

SLIDE WORLD ECONOMIC SUMMIT

HOWZAT **CRICKET** CLUB

FEED-ME

SURF BOARDS

WALK

HIKING EQUIPMENT

Tiptoe & ASSOC.

MOTIVATION EXPERTS

GONE & Co.

BACK IN 10 MINUTES

C.U...

STRIDE HIKERS FOOTWEAR

TRAMPOLINE

CHEQUE BOUNCERS CO-OPERATIVE

PAN

CAMPING SUPPLIES

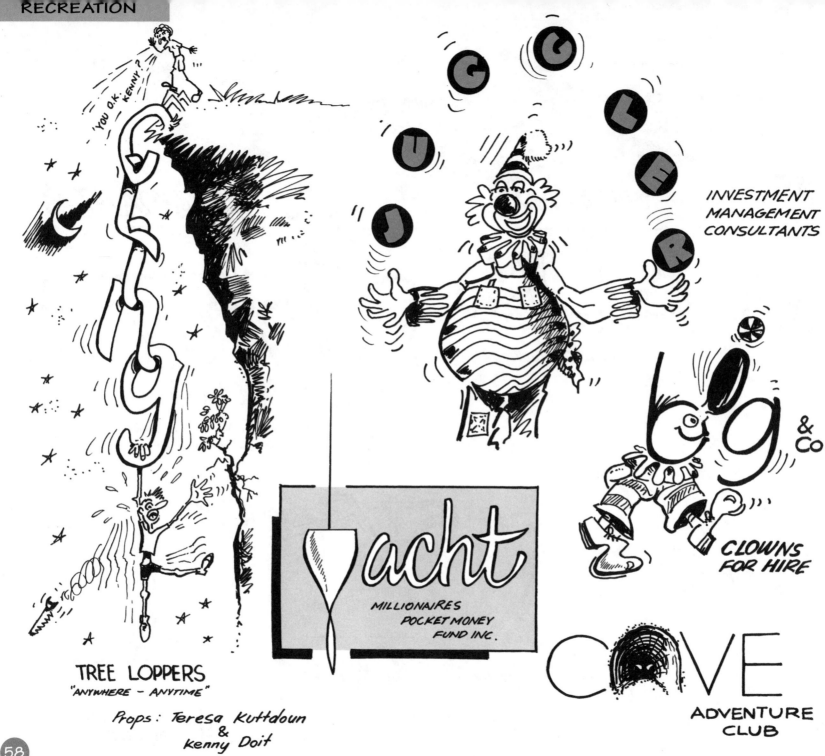

"YOU O.K. KENNY?"

JUGGLER

INVESTMENT
MANAGEMENT
CONSULTANTS

TREE LOPPERS
"ANYWHERE - ANYTIME"

Props: Teresa Kuttdoun
&
Kenny Doit

Yacht
MILLIONAIRES
POCKET MONEY
FUND INC.

bg & Co.
CLOWNS
FOR HIRE

COVE
ADVENTURE
CLUB

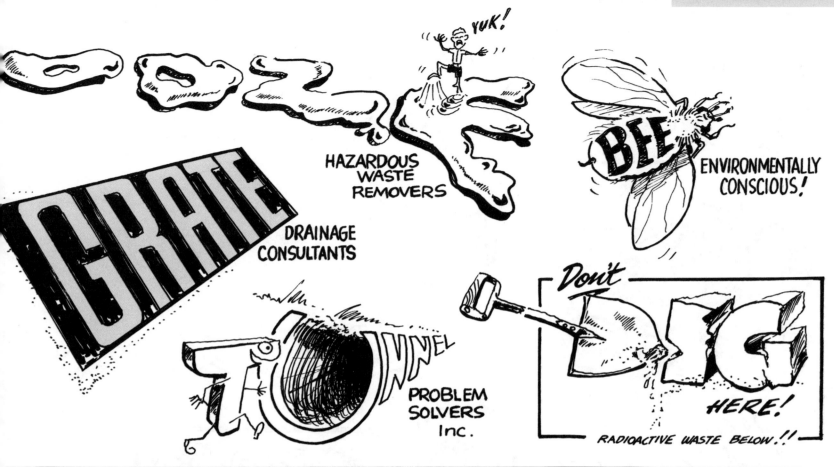

YUK!

HAZARDOUS WASTE REMOVERS

BEE ENVIRONMENTALLY CONSCIOUS!

GRATE DRAINAGE CONSULTANTS

TUNNEL PROBLEM SOLVERS Inc.

Don't DIG HERE! RADIOACTIVE WASTE BELOW.!!

CRAWL & Sons

SEWER-PIPE CLEANERS

population CENSUS COLLECTORS CONSORTIUM Ltd.

spit RETICULATION INSTALLERS

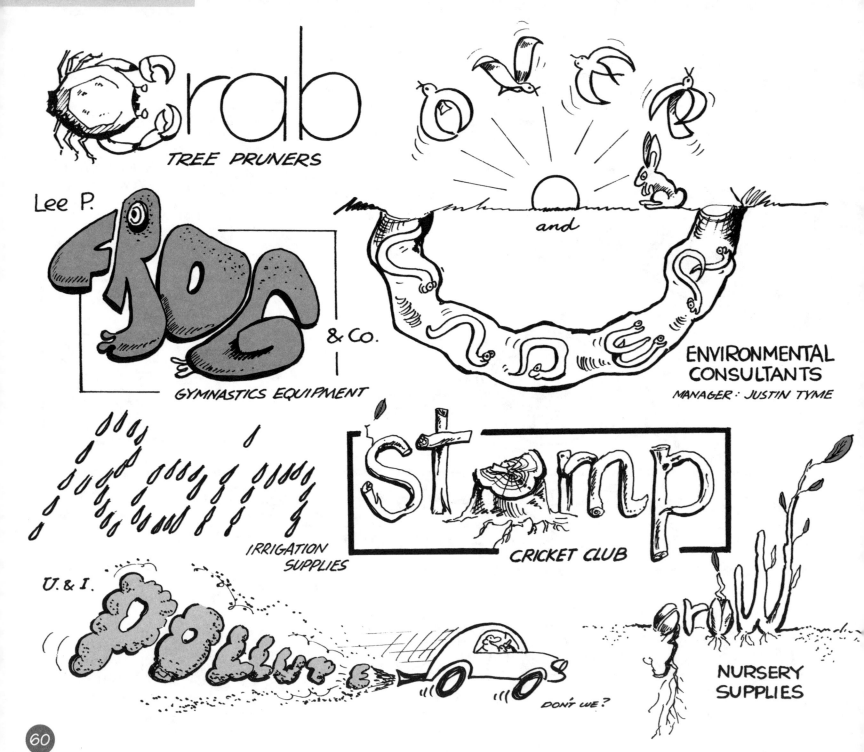

Crab
TREE PRUNERS

Lee P.
FROG
& Co.
GYMNASTICS EQUIPMENT

and

ENVIRONMENTAL
CONSULTANTS
MANAGER : JUSTIN TYME

IRRIGATION
SUPPLIES

stamp
CRICKET CLUB

U. & I.
pollute
DON'T WE ?

grow
NURSERY
SUPPLIES

60

Orchord
Prop: Cherry Ripe

AXE
BUDGET PLANNERS
COMMITTEE

Umbrella & SON
WEATHER FORECASTERS

Vent
FRESH AIR
CONTROL
SYSTEMS LTD.

Teresa Downe & Co.
PAPER
MERCHANT

Junk Yard
Manager: CHUCK OUTTE

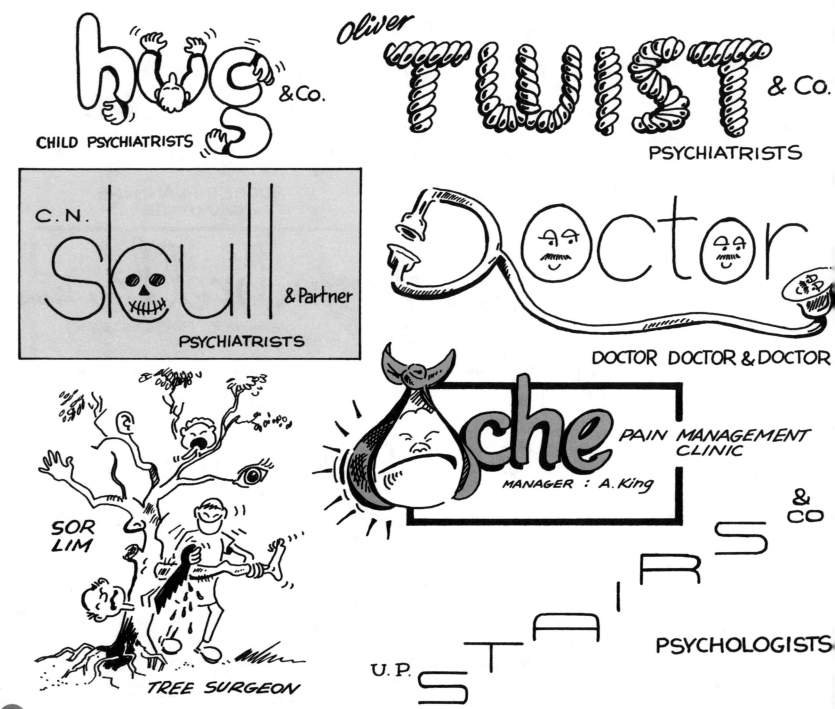

hug &Co.

CHILD PSYCHIATRISTS

Oliver TWIST &Co.

PSYCHIATRISTS

C.N. Skull & Partner

PSYCHIATRISTS

Doctor

DOCTOR DOCTOR & DOCTOR

SOR LIM

TREE SURGEON

Ache PAIN MANAGEMENT CLINIC

MANAGER : A. King

U.P. STAIRS &Co

PSYCHOLOGISTS

To trigger your ideas, just think of

OBJECTS

and ACTION

This will help you bring your projects to life